Sharing Our Stories
in a Shared Space

MW00953562

Stories from Learners of

the Carlsbad City Library

Learning Center Literacy Services

Published by: Lulu.com
Book Cover Design: Deanna Westphal
Photo by: Chris "Shutterhacks" on Flickr
Text Design: Deanna Westphal
Editor: Teresa Brady

ISBN 978-1-300-63090-6
First Edition
Printed in the United States of America

Photos courtesy of the following Flickr users, under the Creative Commons Attribution License:

Dandelion – Lali Masriera – visualpanic
Hallway – Chris – lucidtech
Woman – Alex –eflon
Hands – aussiegall
School – Presagio
Jumping – Marcy Keller – thephotographymuse
Road – Nicholas A. Tonelli – Nicholas_T
Chakras – Hey Paul Studios
Book – >>Zitona<<
Window – Presagio

Eye – Lali Masriera – visualpanic
Milk Jug – aussiegall
Windshield – Robert S. Donovan
Desk – Robert S. Donovan
Liberty – David Paul Ohmer
Navy Ship – Official U.S. Navy Imagery
Daisies – aussiegall
Magnetic Poetry – Steve A. Johnson
Book & Glasses – >>Zitona<<
Sugar Skulls – Mario – mRi

Contents

Foreword

When Carlsbad City Library Literacy Services asked me to write the foreword to this book, I began by reading the stories written by the adult learners who had come from the same learning center where I myself, 25 years earlier, at the age of 48, had taken my first steps to learning how to read and write.

Those of us who have learned to read and write in adulthood have been encouraged by our beloved tutors and literacy providers to tell the stories of our life experiences including our often arduous journeys to literacy. *Sharing Our Stories in a Shared Space* is, in part, a response to these beloved tutors' and literacy providers' requests. It also turns out to be a very important healing experience for the authors, and a declaration by these courageous and tenacious new authors, reminding us all that it is never too late to learn to read and write.

I am convinced that, in America today, it is as important to teach an adult to read as it is to teach a child to read. Learning how to read changes lives and saves lives. Adults actualizing their dreams of learning how to read and write requires tenacity on their part, but it can really only happen with understanding and support of our teachers and communities.

Thank you to the authors for your honesty and creativity. Thank you to the readers for reading these stories and realizing the strength and vulnerability it takes to expose one's own story.

John Corcoran
National literacy advocate, founder of the John Corcoran Foundation, and author of *The Teacher Who Couldn't Read* and *The Bridge to Literacy*

Introduction

This book is a compilation of personal stories written by adult learners from the Carlsbad City Library Learning Center Literacy Services. The idea for this book was born where many great ideas are—at the coffee pot. One day, I struck up a conversation with Teresa Brady, one of our volunteer tutors, and told her it was a dream of mine to publish a book of our learners' stories. Teresa, with the contributions of Literacy Services staff, helped the learners find their writer's voice. The learners responded with their individual stories, and the courage to share them. I hope their words will challenge, move, and inspire you.

Carrie Scott
Community Outreach Supervisor
Carlsbad City Library Literacy Services

Teresa Brady deserves a great deal of credit for her work with the learners. She edited the learners' writing with a light touch, understanding the importance of each word that the learners chose. The staff made minor changes to correct spelling or clarify meaning. In some cases, identifying information of those who are not in our program was changed.

For Carrie Scott, who has devoted the past 25 years to Literacy Services, first as a volunteer tutor, and now as an advocate, coordinator, cheerleader, technology guru, hand-holder, and friend. You are our inspiration.

When Dreams Weren't For Me

Nyla M. Henry

A long time ago someone asked me, "Is there something you have dreamed of doing for a long time?" My answer was, "No, there is not anything I would have done." At the time, I would not have known what steps you even take to fulfill a dream. I had always lived my life in the now. I did not know what it was like to have a dream; my life was about doing what was needed to do to get through it. Dreaming was a luxury that I could not think about. I did do things that I love to do, and things I didn't love to do, but that's how it goes, right?

When I was going to school I was pretty shy and soft spoken. I was afraid of school, the teachers, and the kids. I didn't want my teachers to call on me. I wanted to make myself invisible so I didn't have to take part. My teachers liked me and they moved me along each grade. They did realize however, that I couldn't read (throughout first through twelfth grade) and that I couldn't pass the test to graduate, so they put me in Special Education. My teacher was great, but to me SP-Ed was a holding tank for the bad kids. I did graduate on time, although I still couldn't read. I felt I couldn't go anywhere, I couldn't further my education, and I'd be lucky to find a job above minimum wage.

Dreams weren't for me. I needed to get through each day. I didn't have time to daydream. I met my first husband and had two children. I knew I could be a good mom, although I couldn't cook because I couldn't read the recipes. If we went out to eat and a menu didn't have pictures, I would order whatever someone else had ordered. When I discovered that I couldn't help my kids, I felt crushed. I wanted better for them, but I felt powerless.

My husband never offered any help or encouragement. He was holding my kids back so they didn't dare dream either. I realized I was stuck in a cycle of abuse and low self-esteem and thought it was okay to be the doormat. What I wanted for myself didn't matter. My focus was on how to get through to the next day and how to survive. I was always scared someone was going to find out about my illiteracy and my mistreatment at home. So I had to put on a mask and try to be someone else. Low self-esteem overshadows many adults' desire to learn. We feel we have to do more to prove ourselves. I'm not the only one ashamed of how I was.

I wanted my kids to dream, to believe, and in that desire I realized I wanted a better life for myself too. I needed to break the chain of feeling inadequate. Long story short, I ended my first marriage. I went to work as a janitor and eventually took a job as a property manager. I met and married a loving and supportive man who helped me with all the paperwork (even though he had his own job). After ten years and three employers, the day came when I had to tell my new boss that I couldn't read. Instead of firing me, he told me about Literacy Services. I went and I worked very hard alongside very supportive teachers, bosses and family. I know this may seem simple to most, but it was a daily challenge for me.

I've had the privilege of working with Literacy Services for seven years. Had I not become involved, I would never have acquired the skills or confidence to be sharing my story with you. The tutors and staff have taken time to help me improve my reading, writing and math abilities.

I have applied the tools presented to me to everyday situations: reading street signs, paying bills, cooking from a cookbook and reading a menu in a restaurant. Now I know there is more to life than "hamburger and fries."

I have a better overall understanding of many things now. I am very eager to succeed and I can feel the potential. It's my turn to step up and put out my hand to the person who wants more out of life, the person who wants desperately to change. I am proud to be able to give back to the program by making others aware that help is available to them. I learned to do this as a facilitator for Literacy Services. As a facilitator, I am trained to confidently and effectively educate others who are in need of the services provided.

I can see the effect I am having on my children and grandchildren. My children have become successful readers and are blessed with the gift of being able to read and write. Although my son has passed away, I observed him overcome his learning difficulties and become a competent employee and good father. My grandchildren are learning to read at a very rapid and advanced rate. I feel my being able to read to them and to take part in their lives in this way has had a positive effect on them.

Today I answer the question "Do you have dreams?" much differently. I realize I can dream and I can make those dreams come true. Having the gift of literacy opens many doors and lets me enjoy writings and books that open my mind to the many things I can accomplish now that I have the courage to believe.

The Best Summer Day

Lilia Lopez

I have lived in San Diego for fourteen years and believe it or not, until recently I didn't know about the beautiful and amazing places there are away from North County.

This past summer my family and I decided to do something different besides museums, beaches, water parks, restaurants, shopping, etc. I was looking for an adventure my three children could experience, something new and exciting. At the same time, I wanted something educational and fun.

My husband and I decided we'd go to the mountains for a picnic. Forty-five minutes after packing, we left for Pala. The place was amazing with a great fresh river and many kinds of trees, squirrels chasing about everywhere, kids playing in the river, people sitting, relaxing, and watching the river. Other people were barbecuing, other kids were playing with water toys, and the weather was like a hug telling the people, "Welcome!"

"This is what I was looking for," I said to myself, "a place where you can have fun and be in touch with nature."

Coming to America

Jason Huang

I remember it was at the end of the Chinese New Year in 2008 in Taiwan. My family and I were headed to Taipei airport to take an airplane to the United States. This would be my second trip, but it was the first time for my wife and children.

There were a lot of things to prepare—clothes, books, some daily supplies. The most important thing was our first aid kit. We were not familiar with United States lifestyles. Actually, we knew nothing about America. My wife always said I was either brave or an idiot to go to work in a place we did not know, and especially so to bring my whole family. I considered it an adventure so we packed as much as we could. I think we shipped a total of eight pieces of luggage.

After arriving in Carlsbad, we moved into a big house which belonged to my employer's parent company. It was a really big house with five bedrooms, two living rooms, one dining room and a three-car space garage. It also had a big spa. My kids loved it. It was a good time, but there were some annoying times too. The house was for sale and we had to stay outside on every open house weekend. That was very frustrating.

Three months later, the house finally sold. We moved to the apartment where we currently live. Things went smoothly. The children started school and my wife could buy groceries and food from stores within walking distance. School life for the children was also an adventure for them. They did not know English before coming to the United States. They were like a deaf-mute person because they couldn't understand what they heard and didn't know how to talk so they could be understood.

My daughter explained that the school provided uncooked vegetables and asked how she could eat lunch at school? "It's salad," I told her. "How can I speak to the school to cook salad?" The school's schedule was a problem, too. Kindergarten was from 9:45 a.m. to 1:30 p.m. Elementary school was from 8:10 a.m. to 2:35 p.m. It was very challenging to drop-off and pick-up the children at several times. In Taiwan, I always arranged the drop-off and pick-up at the same time. Taiwan schools expect children to stay at school much longer than here. In Taiwan, school is from 7:30 a.m. to 5:00 p.m. every day.

Cooking styles and materials in our home country are different from the United States. We have to go to San Diego 99 Ranch Supermarket to collect cooking materials once or twice every other week. We usually have a feast when we go to certain San Diego restaurants because we can taste the food we are used to eating.

The weather is comfortable here, the best weather we have ever been to before. In Taiwan, it is hot and humid in the summer season and cold and windy in the winter. In springtime, it always rains, which makes you feel colder.

We love it here even though we are not good enough at English and don't have a lot of friends. We don't know the family cultures, but the people we've met are friendly to us. The education systems here always help us to fit in to the United States. Additionally, the U.S. is a really big country, which means there are more adventures waiting for us.

Las Vegas, a True Story

Linda Peterson

Who said what happens in Vegas stays in Vegas? I do not know, but I do know this is a story that has to be told.

My two sons and I went to Vegas for a few days. We were on the eighth floor at Circus Circus Hotel. It was around 3:20 a.m. on Friday, December 30, 2011 when I heard noises. At first I didn't know if I was dreaming, so I listened carefully. I heard somebody was crying. Somebody was knocking on doors asking for help. When I was completely awake, I opened my door. To my surprise, that somebody was a nine-year-old boy.

I was able to calm him down, and found out his name was Adam. He had come to Vegas with his brother Eli and his father. They were staying in a room just across the hall from us. He didn't know how or what he was doing outside his room at that time. He was very scared. I comforted him and hugged him as if he were my own child. Adam was very happy I was there. We knocked on his door for a while, but nobody answered. I called the front desk. A security guard came to open the door. As soon as the door was opened, my new little buddy jumped on the bed. I covered him and his brother who was asleep on the bed. I noticed his brother Eli was probably not much older than Adam. These two little boys were by themselves. Their father was not in his bed, nor anywhere in the room.

After I put Adam back in bed, I went back into the hall and told the security guard the kids were alone. We came to the conclusion that Adam had been sleepwalking. I couldn't believe no one opened their door to see if they could help. After this episode, I couldn't sleep.

I left the hotel that morning. I don't know if Adam will remember what happened. The incident touched me because the same thing happened to my oldest son when he was nine, the same age as Adam. The difference was that I was there to help my son.

No Greater Love

Claudia Jarquin

The biggest love in the world is the love I met when I had blue days in my life. I didn't know this kind of love existed in this world. How did I discover this love?

One day when I was thinking that I am nobody, not anybody, that I am not good for anything, that I was an estranged person in this world and my life made no sense, I tried to kill myself. While I was working, cleaning on top of the shelves, I saw a big gun. I thought, "There you are. I won't bother with this world anymore." I put the gun to my head, but somebody or something aborted my attempt. I don't know who it was, but something stopped me and I couldn't do it.

There was a second time I wanted to kill myself, but I couldn't do it then either. My life continued and my blue feelings along with it. I was living just to exist. I worked, I talked, I slept and did everything like other people, but I was dead inside. Every day I was deepening and deepening in my sadness and loneliness. At age 14, I started using drugs and alcohol. I was living a bad life. Nobody liked me, nobody loved me. When you are in the darkness, people stay away from you. The only exception was my mom—she loved me so much. It didn't matter who I was, her love was unconditional.

I lived hiding behind my mom. I was a very shy girl. When I turned 16, I started working. My bad habits became worse and worse. I worked at the government office where you can find anything you want, anything you can imagine in this world. I lived this kind of life for many years. I was depressed until one night, while I was sleeping, I had a vision. Jesus came into my dreams. He placed me on a rock and put the rock in His hands, lifting me to the sky, higher and higher. As He began to turn His hand I said, "Lord, please don't let me go down!" He replied, "No more sin, no more sin." I woke up and thought, "Lord, what is this? What do you want from me? What did you want to say to me?"

I tried to be more Christian, more Catholic, but that wasn't the point. The point was that Jesus wanted me to change my life. I didn't understand the message. One day I went to a retreat and people prayed for me. About a week later, while I was at church, I received the presence of the Holy Spirit, although I wasn't really sure what it was. I thought, "What is this?"

I went to confess my sins and I was sweating, crying, and my body felt like it had scars all over it. This lasted for over a week. I started a fight in my dreams during a big, dark, black storm. A strong voice said to me, "You won't change. You're never going to change. You are always going to be what you are." I prayed in my dream and I shouted, "The blood of Christ has power!" I repeated that Jesus Christ's name has power. I felt so strong in my dream. I was the victor in my dream. I shouted, "I have the power!"

When I woke up, I realized Jesus Christ had given me this power. I realized the word Jesus has power and I felt I wasn't alone. I felt He was with me. I didn't know this before receiving the presence of the Holy Spirit. After this dream, I thought I understood the person I was, who I was and where I wanted to go. I thought I understood that Jesus forgave my sins and that I was a new person.

The day I received the Holy Spirit, I called my mom; I called my brothers and sisters to ask their forgiveness. I told them I wasn't in sin anymore. I told my friends, "I am free! I have been reborn. I'm free!" That day was so exciting to me. I felt God's love. I met the grandest love in the world. I thought my mom's love was the biggest love in the world, but now I realized God's love is the biggest. He forgives my sins. He gives me His love. He took care of me when I was in dangerous places practicing bad habits. He took care of me when I slept on the street. He took care of me when I fell down drunk. He was taking care of me when I was alone in my car driving completely intoxicated. He took care of me when I had the gun to my head. He took care of me when I was alone on the street when I arrived in this country and didn't know anybody. Jesus was my savior when people made me work hard and didn't pay me for my job, while they locked me in a room without food, money and family. Who was with me during those bad moments? Only God!

I knew things had to happen to change my lifestyle and to appreciate my creator and my savior. I met the love of God five years ago. He was calling me before, but I couldn't understand His call. My life was very confused when I was living in the darkness of alcohol and drugs. I was living in Mexico City when I developed these bad habits. When I was 20 years old, I started to have dreams with baby Jesus. I'd say, "Please don't cry baby." But I woke up the next day and continued my same routine of alcohol and drugs. The dreams continued until He wasn't a baby anymore. He was like the images I see now of Jesus at age 33. I remember that my mom had a big framed picture with the image of Jesus Christ. In my next dream, I saw Jesus come down out of the frame. He sat close to me and I exclaimed, "Lord, while I am alive, You won't be cold anymore." The image moved back into the frame.

I told my mom about my dream. She only responded, "Oh, how beautiful." I continued partying, dancing, and traveling. My friends and I always traveled around Mexico. Every weekend I took my backpack, threw it over my shoulders and left to any place. I didn't like to stay home even though I had eight brothers and sisters, four boys and five girls in my family. I didn't share much time with them. I'd spend more time with my friends, which was more fun than being with my family (which doesn't mean I didn't love my family).

The drugs and alcohol lifestyle twisted along. One day I returned from a trip to Cancun and I was very tired. We had hitchhiked and it took a very long time, but we got there and back. We had played at the beach in the crystalline water and observed the beautiful multi-colored fish. It was an amazing experience—my eyes popped out of my head. I'd never seen such beautiful water and fish! I fell asleep and had another dream. Again, Jesus Christ appeared. This time He was very angry with me. I saw myself on top of a building that was moving. I was afraid and shouted, "Lord, Lord, help me please! Please don't leave me alone!" Jesus turned His head toward me and turned back, then left.

The building fell down and I jumped off and away from it. I ran away from the demolition. I tried to reach the Lord and His disciples. But it was useless. His disciples said to me, "He doesn't want to talk to you." They turned and left too. I fell down into a big hole of black mud and immediately saw my cousin Angela in that hole, too. I shouted desperately, "No, she is not like me! She is innocent!" Everything seemed useless. Jesus was gone. I climbed out of the hole and woke up.

I wanted to forget that dream because I felt afraid, ashamed, and insecure. I started to drink more than usual and kept driving completely drunk. I remember one day coming out of a bar, it was around two or three o'clock in the morning. I got into my car and drove recklessly, beeping my horn to avoid the oncoming cars. I was passing through red lights on the streets. The police saw me and started to pursue me. "Stop the car!" I heard over their microphone. But I didn't do it because I felt insecure about the police and didn't want them to put their hands on me. I kept driving until I got home. I locked the car and wouldn't get out. The policeman shouted again, "Get out of the car!" I was beeping my horn to get my family's attention, to get them to come out of the house. As soon as I saw everybody coming out together, I got out of the car and ran to my bed. Nobody said anything and the police left after telling my family not to let me out driving again because I might cause an accident.

The next day I went to work, and after my job I went out drinking again. The only thing I wanted was to stupefy my mind with alcohol. I didn't care what people said or how I looked. I didn't have any conscience about what I was doing. I wanted to forget who I was. I was completely confused in my thoughts, in my feelings, and in my whole life. I didn't like the kind of life I was living, but didn't know how to get out of it. The only thing I did was drink and cry. I didn't know what else to do. I died to live.

Five years ago, at Easter during the Passion of Christ, I confessed my sins to the priest in church and recognized the problem I had. When I confessed my sins I again got feverish and my body felt full of wounds. I trembled for almost a week and didn't want to talk to anybody. I still went to work. A couple of months later, my friend Polita invited me to a retreat. People prayed for me. My body started to shake and I began crying from deep within my soul. I shouted, "Thank you Lord!" I felt free of my bad habits. I felt reborn, like something was pulled out from my feet to my head.

Even though I felt free and happy, weeks later I was tempted to go back to my old lifestyle when a friend invited me to go drinking. I drank, but only a few because I felt bad. That night when I went to sleep, Jesus came into my dream. He put me on a big rug and carried me high into the sky. I could feel the breeze on me; I was shaking with fear as Jesus looked into my eyes and said, "No more sin. No more sin." I was very afraid and shouted, "No!" Then I woke up and I was even more fearful. I got down on my knees and I prayed, "Please forgive me dear Lord. What do you want from me? I have nothing to give you. Please forgive me. This won't happen again."

When Jesus took me on the rock, I saw mountains and water. Later on, when I was working in the home of a Jewish family, I saw a big book with "Israel" written in Hebrew across it. When I opened it and scanned through the pages on one page I saw those same mountains I'd seen in my dream! I told my boss, "Look at these mountains. I saw these mountains in my dream." She insisted "No, no, you probably saw them on TV or in a magazine." "No, no, no," I insisted, "The first time I saw those mountains was in my dream!" She turned and left the room.

The word at the bottom of the picture was "Sinai." I became very emotional and closed the book. I had another dream and saw another mountain. It felt like I came out of my body; like I was flying. I started spinning to the inside of the mountain. I saw Jesus and His mother coming towards me. I exclaimed "My dear Lord, my God!" and suddenly I woke up. I wondered, "What was this?" I started attending bible study. When I finished a year later, I said, "Thanks God, no more. I'm done."

I still felt empty inside. I went to another retreat and while at Mass, when the priest raised the chalice, I saw lights flaring like fireworks on the Fourth of July. For five or ten minutes, I was blinded; I couldn't see anything. I covered my eyes and I said, "Oh no, please not my eyes!" I heard a voice say, "Your eyes are my eyes." I answered, "Oh dear Lord, whatever You want from me." I closed my eyes and I could see people around me with their heads covered and their hands over my head. They were praying in a different language. This lasted about 10 minutes. I was afraid to open my eyes. "How will I be able to drive the people who came with me home?" I asked if anybody knew how to drive a stick shift. One of the ladies said, "I can drive, but only if it's an automatic." I told her I could tell her when to change the stick to shift the gears.

As we talked, I shook my head and I could see again. We left and I drove. Back at my house, I said to God, "I don't know what You want from me. I have nothing to give You. I am nobody and I have nothing good in me. I don't understand anything. What can I do with my life now? Before, my life was easy. Whatever I did was okay to me. Now You want to take me to another way and I don't know how to walk this new way. I don't know how to behave. Please show me, Dear Lord."

I began to feel the presence of something. My heart started to feel full. I became an usher at St. Patrick's Church and that made me feel good, like I could do something. The time passed and I continued to feel love in my heart. I confessed that I tried to kill myself. I confessed that I used drugs. I confessed all the bad things I had done before. The priest told me that God loves me; that I don't have to be afraid; that no matter what I did, God's grace was bigger than my sins.

I began living a new life full of love. I recognized His love and His strength for all the creatures He created. Nobody loves me like Him. He shows me His love in every whistle of every bird. He talks to me through the waves in the ocean. He talks to me through the beauty of each flower. He talks to me when the breeze blows across my face. He tells me He loves me when the sunshine warms my body at the beach. I feel His touch when I dive into the water. He says "I love you" when the sun is setting into the ocean. When I open my eyes each morning He says "I love you," and when I see the palm trees blowing during the day. "I love you" is what I hear when the sun shines through the window. While getting out of bed, as I stand up for the day's events, He says, "I love you." This is the biggest love, what God gave us through His son.

One morning I woke up and as I opened my eyes I saw a light by the window. I smiled at the light and I heard a voice say "I love you." I noticed a bird and I heard his whistle as if to tweet "I love you." I went to the beach and observed the ocean, the sky and the sun. I heard the voice say "I love you. I have made all these things for you because I love you." Finally, I could understand how God's love took me out of the black mud. I could understand His love and I thought, "If He made the ocean, the sun, the moon, the stars and everything that exists in this universe, He must be powerful." I recognized how He made everything for me just because He loves me so much. The biggest proof is His son, Jesus Christ, who died on the cross for me.

To me this is real love, the biggest love in the world. Why? Because He forgave my sins; He gave me reconciliation with His father. He loves me without condition and He was waiting for me many, many years until I opened my heart. I realized I couldn't do anything by myself and I said, "Lord, I'm here. I'm all Yours. Do whatever You want with me and my life. I am Yours. You can make me a new human being. Thanks God for Your love. I never thought I could be loved as You love me—to the extreme."

Love is to give your life to others. Now I know what love without condition is. It's Jesus Christ's love.

It's Important to Learn!

Elva B. Mitchell

I came to the United States in 2000. My life was very difficult because I could not speak English very well. I felt miserable, but at the same time, I had confidence in myself. It's time to start to really learn English!

I enrolled in the English as a Second Language (ESL) class at MiraCosta College. I took a test to see how much of my English I speak well. I started at the intermediate level and took the class for almost one-and-a-half years. When I started to work full time, I stopped attending class.

Just about one year ago, I began to study with Literacy Services at the Carlsbad City Library Learning Center. I was assigned a great tutor and a good friend who loves to teach me how to speak and write English. She always tells me I'm doing a great job. She also tells me I'm a good speller. English is very important because it is the only way I can communicate with other people and find a better job.

I'm so glad I came to San Diego to live twelve years ago and decided to learn!

Evolution

Kristin Carro

Over the past ten years, I've had some interesting experiences, like most of us. As I look back on them, I am hoping I have learned some lessons so I will make better choices and decisions going forward.

When I was a junior in high school, I met a boy named Joe. He came up to me and asked if I wanted to go to dinner. Afterwards, we began to hang out regularly. I thought I was in love, and when I graduated I started to work for his mother at a real estate office. My job was to answer phones and file paperwork. Joe wasn't working at that time. He suggested I move in with his family and I agreed. At first, it was great, but it shortly turned for the worst. He began smoking pot. Then he became involved with heavier drugs. Crystal is what I remember. This is when the abuse started.

One night, when Joe was high, he grabbed my hair and pushed me into the bathroom mirror. I have no idea what sparked his action. The mirror shattered. Although I assumed we would get married, he never proposed to me, even when I realized I was pregnant. I decided to abort the baby. Sometimes I regret my choice, and I've shed many tears. I felt it would be selfish to keep the child. The child would suffer because I wouldn't have been able to care for anyone besides myself at that time. I moved out and never contacted Joe again.

I moved in with my parents and enrolled at Palomar College to take a reading class. Soon afterwards, my friend Bev introduced me to Matt. We dated for six months then moved in together. We rented at an apartment complex where I met a boy named Neil and his dog, Cooda. Every day I would walk to the store and back. When Cooda saw me he would run down the little hill and jump up and down for my attention.

One sunny day, Matt and I went to my parents' house. After visiting, we stopped at Vons to buy strawberries. When we got home our apartment door was open and two cops were standing outside. After a 30-minute wait, the policemen let me go in and I could see right away that we'd been robbed. My stuff was scattered all over the place. I filed a police report because I had some very nice, pretty expensive jewelry and my jewelry box had been emptied. The can of money ($400) I kept under my dresser was also gone. (I know, I know. I keep my money in the bank now.) Turns out we had left a window open in the kitchen. The police never found the robber and now I never leave my apartment without making sure the doors and windows are locked.

Matt was working for his stepbrother doing carpet cleaning and wood carpentry. He hated his job. He had a bad temper. He yelled a lot, complained a lot, and drank a lot of beer. When he started abusing me, I made plans to leave. I decided it was not ever going to work out and not the kind of life I wanted to live.

A neighbor told me about Section 8, a program for low-income people. I had to do a lot of paperwork, and it took me four years to get my Section 8 voucher. With the voucher, I got a small apartment and started living by myself for the very first time. I loved decorating my apartment and making it my home. I met some wonderful neighbors—Krissy, Greg, and Dominic—who take me grocery shopping and help me make good food choices. We have meals and barbecues together and that is always fun.

In 2008, I enrolled at MiraCosta College. I also go to Literacy Services for help with my reading, comprehension, and writing. Literacy Services also has a computer class that is helping me with my homework. My tutor told me about a writing class that was being offered at Literacy Services, and I signed up for the class. I enjoy writing and plan to continue writing in the future. Hopefully, my articles and stories will get better and better.

Before going back to school, I didn't know what I wanted to do with my life, but now I do. I know I want to write because I am always happy when my articles are published. Now that I have direction, I also know what I want in a relationship. In the future I hope to meet someone. I am now an independent person and want to meet someone who is mature, has an education, a good job, offers stability, and who treats me respectfully.

A Noble Woman

Claudia Jarquín

Leo was hiding again from her Aunt Lucha to avoid punishment. Leo was very young, and although she was an obedient child, Lucha was abusive towards her and always treated her badly. Leo never said anything to her Uncle Marcos. To avoid punishment, she would hide herself in the house or outside on the patio. When her aunt punished her, she didn't let Leo eat with the family at the table. So Leo would look for potatoes, digging the earth to have something to eat.

Leo was born in the 1930s in Oaxaca, Mexico. She was the eldest of three children in her family. Her sister's name was Maria and her brother's name was Angel. Leo was abandoned by her mother at the age of two, and lived with her Uncle Marcos. She was living in this situation for almost four years, until one day her uncle noticed that

Leo wasn't in the house. He asked his wife where Leo was and she answered, "I have no idea." Marcos started looking for her, but Leo was hiding in panic, so she didn't answer her uncle's calls.

Finally, after a couple of hours, Marcos found her far away from the house. She was shaking with cold. The sunlight was gone and it was dark and chilly. When Marcos found Leo, he hugged her and said, "Everything is okay. Don't be afraid. I will take care of you. Let's go back home." Leo begged in panic, "No, please, I don't want to go back home. Lucha is going to kill me!" "What?!" her uncle exclaimed. He looked at Leo and saw a big injury on her forehead. He asked her what had happened. She started sobbing and told him about Lucha's abuse over the years.

Marcos was very upset when he heard Leo's story and made a decision about Leo's life. When Marcos brought Leo home, he argued with Lucha and packed Leo's clothes to take her to other relatives. Marcos took Leo to Elvira's house, his cousin who lived in Oaxaca. When she got there, she was only six years old. She felt frightened, insecure, and strange. She thought that maybe these people would abuse her, too, when her uncle Marcos introduced her to her other relatives.

However, they were very kind to her and Leo's life started to change, although she still carried emotional scars. One morning somebody sent her to make coffee on the stove, but Leo was too short to reach it. Her foot got stuck, and she fell down and the hot coffee spilled on her. It wasn't her fault, but she didn't know that at the time. She was panicked and ran away to hide. She hid in the attic. Leo imagined that people's reaction to her mistake would be bad. Leo couldn't think because she was too little to think. She tried to save her life because she thought, "If Lucha abused me for nothing, now they are going to kill me for this." She went up to the attic; she felt safe there.

When Elvira asked where Leo was, somebody said, "She went to put the coffee on." "What?!" Elvira exclaimed, "Who sent her to put the coffee on?" No one knew. Elvira shouted, "Go look for her and bring her to me right now." Everybody went to the kitchen yelling, "Leo, Leo where are you?" Leo was on top of them looking at what was happening. All the family was looking for her, until one of them looked up and saw her. "Here she is. Come down, little girl." They took her to Aunt Elvira who asked her, "Are you okay? Did you burn yourself?" Leo was shaking, she was mute; she was panicked and couldn't stop crying. They took her to the doctor. Fortunately, she was okay. After that incident, Leo's family took better care of her.

Leo's life continued until she met Pedro when she was seventeen years old. Pedro came to work with his uncle Fortino, who was Elvira's husband. Leo and Pedro were engaged for one year. After their marriage, Pedro became violent and Leo suffered a new Calvary as Pedro's wife. Pedro abused her physically and verbally during their marriage. He never gave her enough money for their children, so Leo had to work hard every morning selling vegetables and every afternoon washing people's clothes. In addition to her work, she was raising nine children. She never let others take care of her children, but brought them with her everywhere. They were like little ducks following their mother.

Leo's happiness in life was her love for her children and their love for her. She lived only for them, and endured the marriage for their welfare. She lived with Pedro for forty years and, when she was sixty years old, found the strength to leave him because she felt that her life was really in danger. She was so strong; it was the most difficult decision in her life.

Today, Leo is seventy-nine years old. She has nine children, seventeen grandchildren and thirteen great grandchildren. Leo is still a hard worker and she is still helping her children. She is an amazing mother, and I know this because she is my mother. Proudly I say, "This is my mother." I thank God who gave me this beautiful mother. I couldn't imagine having a different mother. She doesn't have much education and does not know how to read or write, but she does know how to open her heart and be available to love those who are around her. My mother taught us the most important lessons in life by her own example. She taught us how to love. She taught us how to forgive. She taught us to be honest and to respect and be of service to others. In spite of her own suffering and abandonment, she showed us how to be thankful to God and not take His gifts for granted.

This is what my mother taught me. If she were here with me, I would tell her how much I love her and say, "Thank you, Mom, for loving us and for being such a loving example. I love you, Mom, with all my heart."

Success is to be measured not so much by the position that one has reached in life as by the obstacles which he has overcome. -Booker T. Washington

My Turning Point

Lupe Green

When I was introduced to Reiki, my life changed. Reiki is a Japanese spiritual practice. It is done by a palm healing and, it is believed, heals with one's self energy. As I was learning the art of Reiki, I was able to see and feel differently, experiencing things that had happened to me in my dreams and during daydreams, things about which I had no understanding. With the help of Reiki, it all came together. Reiki has opened up energy paths, bringing knowledge and understanding. It has helped me spiritually.

One of the benefits of Reiki is to explore one's chakras. Chakras are made up of seven points in our body which are believed to be the main sources of healing for our organs. The first chakra is red, located at the perineum (base). The second is orange, located at the lower abdomen (sacral). The third is yellow and is located on our stomach (solar plexus). The fourth chakra is green, located at the heart. The fifth is blue, located at our throat. The sixth is indigo, located at the top of the head (third eye). The seventh chakra is violet and is located at the crown.

Each of these chakras has special healing components. In order to open each of these chakras and connect with their power, you need to be in a deep state of relaxation. After meditation, you'll feel full of energy.

I have acquired more patience and understanding, along with a stronger love for God, which I apply to my daily life and practice. I am very happy about all that I have learned. Hopefully, it brings healing and health to others as well.

Rebecca's Story

Rebecca N. Flores

My name is Rebecca N. Flores. To my friends I am known as Remi. I was born on November 24, 1992. Ever since I can remember I have always had a problem with learning, but I didn't know what was wrong. My whole life has been trying to blend with everyone else, but due to this problem I could not. No one knew what it was. I could not get help. I felt like I was given up on due to this. Through many years of difficulties I have learned to teach myself to read and write, but sadly my skills are not as good as they should be. I used guessing; listening mostly. Whatever I would hear I would think it would be the word. That was hard. Teachers gave up on me. They thought I was lazy or just wasn't trying. I was depressed and lonely. There were some nurses who believed there was something wrong, which was a relief. At least some people believed me.

One day in my third year of high school, my teacher, Ms. Gaitan, told me there was a testing program I should try. I was diagnosed with Irlen Syndrome[*]. When I was tested, I was found to have the worst symptoms of anyone in all of the classes. That's when the door opened up for me. My world changed from one direction to another. I actually understood me for the first time in my whole life. I felt I was like everyone else, that there was nothing wrong with me anymore.

The symptoms I suffered over the years were headaches and light sensitivity, to the point that after a few minutes of class I would get sick to my stomach and have to be sent home. This was very difficult for me for so many years. My whole life, teachers did not believe me when I told them my symptoms. They were unusual symptoms to have all at once, so no one knew what I had. I was tested for dyslexia and ADD, but because I didn't test positive for either of these, they thought I was making it up. Now I know what Irlen Syndrome is and I use the Irlen overlays every day of my life.

After college I am hoping to get into theater and become a voice actress. I adore theater. I just love it. I love to perform. I love to act. Because of Irlen Syndrome, when I was growing up, learning lines and memorizing them was hard for me. I would always forget my lines. Teachers would never understand why it would take me so long to learn my lines. It would take me a month to memorize what everyone else did in a week. Once I got the overlays, I could remember my lines much faster. I felt proud of myself on stage because it only took me a week to memorize the lines that used to take me a month. I know that if I work really hard and have lenses, I will be able to achieve my dream.

At a young age I tried to play the violin. The notes would move around on the page and my teacher would never understand it. It took me three years to learn "Twinkle, Twinkle, Little Star" on the violin. Over time it wasn't worth it. I didn't know about Irlen Syndrome then. I couldn't take the pain of headaches and migraines, so I gave up the violin. This disability might have taken a lot from me over the years but, thanks to the overlays, I am finally taking them back one by one.

After I got my overlays and a couple days after my grades improved, I noticed my brother had some of the same symptoms I had. Teachers didn't believe him either. He was 11 years old. I took him to be tested, and it turned out he had Irlen Syndrome as well. His grades are improving now, too. Seeing this and seeing how hardly anyone knows about it, I have decided to make another goal in life—to spread the word around so that someday it will be known across the entire world. I want to share my story to reach others who might have this disability.

My new dream is that someday Irlen Syndrome will be tested for in all schools, and no child will have to face what I had to face. I want people to know about Irlen Syndrome so that teachers can be more understanding and not discouraging to kids who have it.

*To learn more about Irlen Syndrome, visit www.irlen.com

I Am Worth It!

Nyla M. Henry

My life changed once I made the decision to learn how to read and write. I feel more confident and I'm less dependent on my family, yet I feel closer to them. Since becoming an adult learner in Literacy Services at the Carlsbad City Library Learning Center, I'm no longer embarrassed. I have moved from wanting to hide to wanting to participate because "I am worth it."

Until the age of 40, I wasn't able to read or write. I can remember back when I would go out into the world feeling unworthy and very lonely—for a long time! It is amazing to me that I can now write and read what I write, and other people can read it, too (like you right now!). I can even share my story with small and large groups of people I don't know. It may be difficult at first, but it builds my courage and my determination. The people who congratulate me make it all worthwhile. I do run into those people who can't believe my story. It's just that they are in denial of things they don't know or understand.

Now look at me! I can read a book on my own—and comprehend it. It is unbelievable how much the world has opened. I needed to speak out about my feelings of inadequacy and low self-esteem. Knowing your true self is a lifelong process. I know now that while I was waiting on someone's help, I was waiting on me. I was waiting on me to make the decision to either pursue the life that was meant for me or be stifled by the one I was living. I realized that I am worth each moment that I put time into myself.

What is the truth of your life? It is your duty to know. The truth is what feels right. The truth allows me to live every day with integrity. Everything that I do and say shows the world who I really am. By living my journey, I am letting myself be heard in so many ways. I believe unmasking the shame has set me free.

Did you know that when you can't read or write it's a very lonely and scary place for you to be? I know that when I didn't have the skills to communicate, that my world was a different place. I finally became ready to tell the truth and shout "I am worth it!" I was finally ready to walk through that door not knowing how it would turn out, but I was willing to take the risk. I am more confident now than ever. I am less dependent. I am not ashamed of myself any longer. Since I've been a learner, I now know there's hope and that not feeling worthy doesn't have to overshadow me. Believing in yourself is trusting in yourself. It is incredible how much I have changed for the better. I did break that feeling of inadequacy. I just needed to love myself and come to understand that "I am worth it!"

A Scary Beginning

Hermond E. Jones

When I completed my boot camp training at Great Lakes, Illinois, I could take several days of leave before reporting to my next duty station. So once my furlough was approved, I took seven days of leave. It was a good thing I did!

Ready to report for duty, I took the Greyhound bus from Newark, New Jersey to Washington, D.C. where I transferred to another Greyhound bus going to the naval station in Norfolk, Virginia. When I departed from that bus at the naval station, a Navy bus was waiting for us to take the sailors around the pier where our ships were docked. The driver dropped me off at Pier 12.

"That's your ship, straight down that pier," he said. I gathered up my sea bag and the small suitcase I had brought with me from home with my personal things. Arriving at the bottom of the ladder, I looked up toward the quarterdeck. I heard a voice way up there saying to me, "Sailor come aboard." I was so afraid of what might happen after I reached the top of the ladder. I was in for a real surprise that Saturday afternoon.

It was after 5:00 p.m. when I arrived at the ship and I will tell you or anybody I had the worst time checking in at my new duty station. Only the duty section was aboard. The rest of the ship's crew was off on liberty for the weekend. Getting assistance from the duty section personnel was like trying to find a dentist's office open after 5:00 p.m. The duty Master-at-Arms took me to my assigned living quarters and returned to his office. About one hour later he came back with a blanket-and-sheet roll that smelled like someone homeless had been sleeping on it for weeks. The duty Master-at-Arms said to me, "The Chief Master-at-Arms has the key to the sheet and blanket locker. Therefore, you're out of luck in getting a clean set until Monday morning."

The first thought that went through my mind was, "What have I gotten myself into?" By now I was several decks below the water line and it was creepy and scary to me. The duty Master-at-Arms told me, "The only lights below deck are red lights, except in the passageways, where there are white lights until Taps, at 10:00 p.m." Once I entered the berthing space I felt like I was headed into the red-light district of lower Manhattan. I got an awful feeling about the place and what might be going on down there, and what might happen to me sleeping in a place like this. Then the duty Master-at-Arms said, "Bunk number twenty is your rack."

As I was unpacking my sea bag, one of the young sailors walked by and said, "You came to the wrong place, especially because you're a Black man." Here I was coming from New Jersey, thinking everything was going to be all right. I had not eaten since I left the Greyhound bus station in Washington, D.C., about four hours earlier. I asked the duty Master-at-Arms about getting some food. He told me the galley was closed and there wouldn't be any food available until Sunday morning at 7:45 a.m. I only had a few coins in my pocket so I couldn't even go to the snack machine. I was hungry and completely lost, and I did not know how to get back to the quarterdeck or the entrance to the ship.

It was an experience no young sailor should have to go through in the beginning of his Navy career. The first few hours onboard had given me a chilling feeling and serious worry about the rest of my military career. It took me two hard weeks aboard the ship to make adjustments and start living the shipboard life.

Still Confused But Grateful

Lilia Zamora

At the very early age of 17, after my mother's death, I was completely responsible for taking care of my three younger sisters, ages 7, 9 and 11. My father and three brothers, along with two older sisters, had departed for America years earlier, so it was up to me to fill this void. It was up to me to take full responsibility for caring for their needs, including their education. Since I had to work to help support my sisters, I was unable to complete my education after the ninth grade. I was unable to complete high school, which I had so wanted to do. This was when I realized how difficult it was for my mother to be independent all those years, raising a family all by herself.

After age 19, my brothers decided to help me come to America to find a better life. My dad had finally returned home and was around to help my three younger sisters who remained in Mexico. I was in a strange country with no knowledge of the English language, so my first work opportunity came as a hotel housekeeper and then as a factory assembly worker in Carlsbad. At this time, I realized the importance of learning English in order to survive in a new country so I began English classes next to our Carlsbad Senior Center.

Soon after, I married and later had my first son. I became too busy working and caring for my family to learn English. When my second son was born three years later, I became even busier. When my sons began junior high school I knew I had to find the time to continue with English classes to be able to communicate with their teachers and help them with their classes.

Years ago I had heard about Literacy Services, a literacy program for adults, and I had always desired to sign up. My fear was that they would not accept me. However, about three years ago one of the librarians accompanied me to an interview and I was able to participate. It gave me joy to be accepted into this program because it made me feel so much safer.

Even today, I am still confused with the English language, but it's no longer totally strange to me. I am much more comfortable now being able to communicate with someone who helps make the language a bit more familiar. It is making a great difference in my life every day. I am very grateful and thankful for people who are willing to sacrifice their time and energy in order to give people like me hope for a better opportunity for a better future.

My Family Traditions

Catalina Lopez

My family has really important traditions. One of them is the reunion of family members, including grandparents, uncles, aunts, cousins, nephews, sisters and brothers. At our birthday parties we all have very much fun.

When somebody in the family has a problem, we help that person. Another tradition is *Las Posadas* at Christmas. We make tamales, champurrado and a piñata for the kids. After that we give candy bags for the people.

Another celebration is *El Dia de los Muertos*. We take a bunch of flowers and crowns of flowers to the tombs of loved ones. We also make altars for the deceased people, placing their favorite foods, for example, mole, beer, bread, tamales and Coke, on the altars.

Another tradition that some families celebrate is a big party for the girls who are becoming 15 years old. It is a Quinceañera. We attend a Mass and afterwards we have food and each of the girls dances a waltz with the court or young man of honor. They wear beautiful dresses, some like Cinderella's. It is a nice celebration.

My Borrego Desert Adventure

Nieves Moran

Some years ago, I was without work, and as the weeks passed, I began to worry how to cover my expenses. One day I was talking with a friend, and mentioned that I had no work and only one interview in the near future. She told me that she was working with three older people, a mother and her two daughters. She didn't go into great detail, except to say that the work was going well.

A week passed and my friend, Phyllis, called to ask me if I had gotten work. When I said I had not, she asked if I wanted to work for a week as her substitute. The family lived in Borrego Desert, and Phyllis was sick and did not want to travel so far. The work involved taking care of the family's mother. I said yes, so Phyllis told me to go to an appointment the following Monday.

I packed my suitcase with enthusiasm, let another friend know where I would be, and traveled to meet the family for the first time. I left that day without knowing much about the family or the situation, but happy to have a job.

When I arrived, I was introduced to the younger sister, Lucy. That was my first surprise. Lucy, you see, was eighty-three years old—and she was the younger sister. Her older sister Nancy was eighty-five and their mother was one-hundred-and-five years old. At first I thought, "What am I going to do?" But the work was easy, and the mother was very happy with my care and very nice. All went well for the first three days, until dinner on the fourth day.

I had noted that everyone in the family was very fond of drinking wine, and consumed about a bottle a night. The wine itself was not the problem, but the combination of wine and the various prescription medicines they all took daily caused them to constantly quarrel with one another.

After dinner that night, the sisters stayed in the kitchen and I went to prepare their mother for bed. All of a sudden, I heard screams coming from the kitchen, and, when I arrived, I saw blood everywhere—it was on the cabinet, on the floor and Nancy's leg was covered in it. Because the sisters argued so much, at first I thought, "No! Is it possible that these two eighty-something-year-old women were fighting with each other?" As it turned out, Nancy had hit her leg on the open dishwasher, causing a nasty-looking wound.

At first, Nancy tried to treat her wound with first aid, because she did not want to call 911. She could not stop the bleeding, though, and she and Lucy became very nervous. They finally called the emergency number and an ambulance arrived with paramedics. Then the police arrived, which was a surprise.

As the paramedics began to treat Nancy's leg, they asked what had happened. She explained that she forgot the dishwasher door was open and she hit her leg on it. One of the policemen asked her the same question, and wanted to know how many people were in the house. Nancy told him there were four women, and then he said they would have to check the house. It appeared the police did not believe Nancy, and seemed suspicious of the big bottle of wine on top of the table. Why would these three older women have such a big bottle?

The police proceeded to look carefully in every room in the house. They explained they were looking for someone hiding in the house, someone who might have caused Nancy's injury. After they found no one, the police began to interrogate me. They asked so many questions. Who was I? Why was I here in the house? Where was I from? Did I have identification? They even checked my breath; they made me open my mouth and shone a light in it to see if I was drinking. They made me very nervous with their questions because, at the time, I did not understand much English and I was afraid they might decide to put me in jail.

The police proceeded outside the house and waited while Nancy and her sister went to the hospital. I stayed with their mother, who was asleep and not aware of all the activity. Nancy was at the hospital for a long time, and her mother woke up and said, "I want to see Nancy." I told her Nancy was at the store—even though it was around midnight—so she went back to sleep. More time passed and the mother woke again, saying "I want to see Nancy." So I told her again Nancy was at the store, because I did not want to upset her. But the third time she woke she said, "Nancy has been at the store a long time." So I had to tell her the truth.

Suddenly, the mother got out of bed, grabbed her walker and started for the door. Halfway there, she lifted her walker over her head like a weightlifter and brought it crashing down. For two hours she was weightlifting her walker as though she was in training for a gold medal at the Senior Olympics. I was astonished at her strength and stamina. Then she started to scream, "Where is my Nancy?"

This screaming and crying made me so nervous, because I thought for sure the police would come running in and find me with a one-hundred-and-five year old woman and think that I was doing her harm. I tried to calm her, but she kept shouting for Nancy and crying. Finally, Nancy and Lucy arrived home and reassured their mother that Nancy's leg would be fine.

The next day I packed to return to San Diego and felt so relieved to have survived this adventure. I could not wait to leave. During our farewell, Nancy told me how grateful she was for my help, that everyone liked me and my work and offered me a permanent job with their family. I said, "Thank you very much, but I have an interview for another job waiting." What I immediately thought was, "If I stay here one more night, they'll have to put me in the funny farm." It was clear to me that, if I worked for this family, I would certainly not reach one-hundred-and-five-years old. This job would considerably shorten my life.

I Will Never Give Up

Carmen Cordero

I remember growing up in the Dominican Republic and going to the public school. One of my teachers noticed I was behind the other kids when we were doing spelling tests and writing small sentences. I kept missing a lot. During the day she would test me and I almost always missed the same work. My writing was so jumbled I couldn't even read my own words. I repeated second and third grade twice. My third grade teacher sent a note to my parents to come to talk to her.

The teacher recommended to my mom that I attend a special school where they had maybe ten children in the classroom. It was called something like Centros de Rehabilitación. My mom hired a lady, Luisa, to help me with spelling and writing. However, I was not interested. I was mean to her. I'd throw things on the floor. She'd repeat a word many times, but I wasn't getting anywhere. I just wanted to play with my friends. My mom ended up putting me in the special school. I was about ten years old.

It was hard because most of the people who were there looked developmentally disabled. Some had physical problems too. One student was missing a hand, another missing a leg. I remember specifically a girl who became a friend. Her name was Rosita and she had one hand that she couldn't open. She also limped when she walked. I was ashamed of myself for thinking I wasn't a normal person and that was why I couldn't attend a regular school. I looked perfect to the outside world, but I knew I wasn't going anywhere with my writing and reading. One of the most embarrassing things about going to that school was when they had to pick me up at my house or drop me off. I could hear some of the neighborhood kids making fun of me. They would call me retarded.

Shortly after I started at the special school my mom moved to Puerto Rico and I stayed with my aunt in the Dominican Republic. My mom came back often. The reason my mom moved away was because she wanted to have a better future for the family. She was trying to get all of her children (my brother, my sister and me) to become residents of the United States. I missed my mom but she did what she needed to do.

Meanwhile, I stayed at the school and learned enough to just get by. I learned little tricks such as how to sign my name, read signs and do math. It took me awhile, but I did it. Beside regular school they had cooking class, taught sewing and even how to become a hairdresser or a mechanic. It was a vocational school which I attended for three or four years. I always paid attention whenever I went any place so

I would have landmarks. Even though I couldn't read the name or address on a place, I would know how to give directions by telling the color and what the surroundings were.

When I was about 13 or 14, my mom sent for us and we moved to Puerto Rico. She did it! She brought my brother, my sister and me and we became U.S. residents. (My father never came to the U.S.) I attended school in Puerto Rico where they had better things and I learned a little bit more. But I still found myself most of the time behind everyone else. I couldn't keep up with the other students. Even though school was in Spanish it was hard for me to put a letter together to my friends, my father, etc. I did my best, but I missed a lot of words.

When I was 17 I dropped out of school to get married to someone in the Dominican Republic. Looking back I think I was too young and too confused. Anyway, I was working at this time in a factory and going to school at night and helping my husband get his papers to become a legal U.S. resident. After his papers came through he moved to Puerto Rico and soon after that he moved to New York hoping to find a job so that we could reunite since I was still in Puerto Rico. We would see each other rarely. I eventually moved myself to New York and quickly found a job. My husband and I finally got to live together for a month or two. He was not successful in finding a job so I was supporting him. I realized I wanted more for me and that the marriage was not working, so we divorced.

I never went to school in New York. It was hard for me to live in New York because of the weather and the crime. One day I was coming home from visiting someone in the Bronx and as I got out of the subway train a woman came up to me, grabbed my purse and held a knife to my face. I let her take my purse. I was shaken, but alive. Also, coming from the Caribbean I needed a warmer climate.

By this time my sister was living in California and I decided to come to California, hoping it would be safer and warmer. This was the best thing I have done for myself. Many doors opened for me. I lived with my sister for a while. I also worked at Children's Hospital Orange County (CHOC) doing housekeeping. I learned a lot there and applied for a nurse's aide position when it became available. I got that position.

I started dating a man, Joe, who was very encouraging and helpful about my studying and my problems. He encouraged me to speak English and attend ESL classes. I went to Vista High School and took English classes there and special classes for nursing, first aid, etc. I also went to the program at MiraCosta College for disabled students taking English and Math classes. The classes were all small. I was tested to see what my problems were and it turned out that I have dyslexia. I was also told that I was the type of learner who needed to see things in order to learn and practice them so I could comprehend them.

I eventually married Joe. He also told me about Literacy Services offered by the Carlsbad City Library Learning Center. I called the library and spoke to Lynda who was in charge then. I met with her and she gave me an evaluation test. I was put on a waiting list and eventually she found a tutor for me. I have been involved with Literacy Services for about ten years now, and I have to say this has been the second best thing that has happened to me. It has been a long journey for me, but it is worth it. I will never give up.

Freak Accident

Gary Hailstone

Have you ever been at fault in a car accident? Have you ever been afraid of having to pay for the damages of multiple cars and property? Have you ever been nervous about people yelling at you at the scene? Have you ever been anxious about whether your insurance would cover it all? Have you ever had pangs of conscience about what to do? Six or more years ago, I decided which motorists of several I would help. This decision has stayed with me.

I was on my way home, driving my work truck in the middle lane on I-5 South near San Onofre. As I drove, the truck's drive shaft suddenly snapped in three and parts ended up in several lanes of the freeway. Cars were swerving out of the way of the objects, but some cars did hit them and it put a gash in their tires. Those cars had to pull over and I had to choose which car with a flat tire to help. I was nervous. I didn't want anyone to find out it was my fault. I didn't want people to be mad at me, plus I was scared about what my insurance company would do.

Even in a crazy situation on the side of the freeway, I was able to remain calm enough to choose a family who appeared to need the most help. I walked up and said, "Hello. Do you need any help?" They were from out of state, on vacation and going to Sea World. The wife was already out of the car and looking at the tire. She was going to try to fix the flat tire herself, but I could tell she needed assistance. She was wondering how she would be able to do this with her family in the car. She looked at me with a blank stare and said, "I'd be very grateful if you could help me fix my flat tire. I ran over someone's car parts and now there's a gash in the side of my tire."

I changed the tire on the family's rental car. The dad was disabled and the mom was concerned about doing it on her own as the cars were driving by. The family was very grateful that I came over to assist them. They offered me money, but I denied the "reward" and just took it as a good deed. I did admit to them that it was my drive shaft that did the damage to their rental car.

I didn't tell any of the other stranded drivers that it was my car's parts that caused their inconvenience. I was worried I would have to show my license and insurance card, and that they might make claims. As I looked around, the other cars had people to change their tires so they could continue up the road. If I am ever put in this situation again, I would do the exact same thing in choosing the car that needed the most help.

Actually, a couple of weeks ago, I was put in a similar predicament during a freeway accident. This one wasn't my fault, but I was at the scene so I stopped and took the opportunity to help out. It was a good choice six years ago and today because I like to be responsible for helping others.

My Favorite Memory

Nyla M. Henry

My best memory is treasure hunting with my dad. We would go out to the riverbed and dig up small treasures from the past. The best treasure was an antique gentleman's mirror. It had three framed mirrors which were fused together. The back side was covered with leather carvings and it had a long chain to hang or place on a flat surface. In the past, men would hang their mirror on a tree or on their wagons during their travels. The ladies would put them on their tabletops.

My dad and I would come back with the coolest things. We'd go out to the riverbed and dig until we'd find something, things like milk jugs, dolls and medicine jars. You could see his excitement in the way my dad talked about our findings. Our treasures were actually the personal belongings of the people traveling in covered wagons from the east to the west. My dad and I loved the hunt. We just never knew what we would find.

For me, this will always be a special memory because I love history and it tied me to the past. It was as if my dad and I were on this incredible adventure together.

My First Adventure

Linda Peterson

I was 15 years old and it was the beginning of my last year at Antonio Barbosa Heldt Junior High School. A program named CONAFE (Consejo Nacional de Fomento Educativo) arrived at our school.

My school was in the town of Armería, which is approximately an hour bus ride from my village Coalatilla. My village was very small, about 500 people, and only had an elementary school, so to go to junior high or any higher level of education was a big thing. Not many had the opportunity, not because of the high cost. Sometimes, like in my case, my father didn't want me to go to school. He never gave me a good reason why. I think he just wanted to show that he had the control. My father was an alcoholic and verbally and physical abused my mother and all my brothers and sisters (eight of us). My mother and my oldest brother supported me and ignored my father when he was in the house. I had to be very silent and not turn the lights on in our one-room house when I was leaving for school. I'd get up at 4:30 a.m. and walk to the park where the bus would pick me up. I'd hide my uniform under a blanket and dress in the dark. My brother would ride from work on his bike to wait for me at the bus stop to escort me home to make sure my father was not around to punish me for not obeying him. After three years, I finished junior high school.

I signed up for CONAFE because the program gave teens like me the opportunity to teach kindergarten in rural places for one year. In return, we would earn a high school scholarship. The program required that I attend training every Saturday from 8:00 a.m. to 5:00 p.m. for a whole year. I learned how to teach children to write their names, numbers from 1 to 20, the alphabet, and the vowels. They taught me how to motivate the kids so they'd enjoy going to school.

I recall my last class when the teacher showed us a list of possible places where we could be sent. I was very excited when I was told I'd be going to the farthest place on the list. My first reaction was "Oh my God!" They sent me to a very remote village. I don't even remember its name. It was hidden in the mountains of Manzanillo Colima.

When I first arrived, I conducted a census, going house to house to find out how many children were old enough to attend kindergarten. They had to be five years old on the first day of school. We couldn't teach if there were less than five or more than 15 kids. As it turned out, there were not enough eligible children.

I had to wait until the next day to take the bus back to the city of Manzanillo. It was a little scary to stay with people I'd never met before, but to my surprise, they were very respectful. It was the rainy season and it rained all night long and a few more days. The river was flooded, so I had to stay six more days until we could cross the river.

Since there were not enough children in the village, they sent me to another village named El Alpuyequito which wasn't too far from the city of Colima. This smaller place had a tiny classroom and I started teaching five kids. We were having a good time; I got to know my students' parents very well. When one of the kid's parents went to live in another place, I had to move again to another town. Finally, I was sent to a place called La Loma which means "the hill." It was situated in the mountains of Colima, bordering the State of Jalisco. La Loma was surrounded by small hills and big mountains. It had a huge river that provided water to the community and to the farmers.

As soon as I arrived, I felt a connection with these surroundings. It was beautiful and my first thought was "I belong in this place." I immediately moved in to the Comisario's house as I was supposed to, then I did the census. There were 12 kids to teach. I felt relieved. I remember arriving on a Friday. After I got settled, I went to check the classroom. I wanted to make sure everything was clean and ready to go on Monday. On the first day I called the name of each student. All my 12 kids were on time. Like me, they were very excited. I felt I had a huge responsibility to those enthusiastic new learners. I promised myself to enjoy my experience as a teacher.

People from La Loma were very poor. They sustained themselves from the crops they planted, such as corn, beans, rice, and seasonal vegetables. Some of the parents raised cattle, pigs, chickens and goats. Each of the students' parents was required to provide me food each week. I would rotate every week to another child's house. I remember in some houses I ate eggs for breakfast, lunch and dinner.

On weekends I would return to my home in Coalatilla, leaving Friday afternoons and returning Sundays. It was hard because only one bus went back and forth from Colima City to La Loma and the trip took an entire day, one way. I decided not to go home every weekend when the program started having meetings in Tecomán on the last Friday of every month to report the progress of each child. Since this was closer to Coalatilla, I'd leave Thursday after school and take three buses to arrive at my aunt's house where I'd stay the night. After Friday's meeting I'd journey on to Coalatilla to see my family.

Once I missed the bus in Colima. I don't remember if I arrived late or the bus was broken and never came. I had to take another bus to the closest town then wait to see if anybody with a car going in my direction came along so I could get a ride. It was getting late and no one passed. I decided to walk, faster and faster. It took me hours to get to La Loma. I was exhausted because I was carrying all my stuff, a backpack and a small suitcase. I learned my lesson and the bus never left without me again.

During my time in La Loma, I introduced the people in the town to two new events. The first was the Queen of Spring celebration. In Coalatilla, this event occurred every year on March 21st, the first day of spring. The purpose of the Queen of Spring festival was to raise money to improve the quality of the classroom and to buy school supplies. All my students' parents agreed to help me with everything.

The people had never had a spring festival before, and they were excited. All the girls in my class competed for the honor of being the Queen, who was chosen by a vote of the whole class. It just so happened that the prettiest and nicest girl in the class won. I trained the winning little girl how to wear heels and how to walk to look like a real queen.

It took two months of preparation. Because La Loma was so small, we made posters inviting people from surrounding towns. La Loma had a cement court which was used for big events. I contracted a band from Tecomán to perform. It took some work to track them down and I had to talk them into getting paid after the event and receiving a percentage of the sales. People volunteered to clean the court, and to hang all the multi-colored crepê flowers the children and I made. The fathers were in charge of cleaning the tables and chairs and making sure that the drinks were in the coolers. The students' moms were in charge of making food to sell during the event. They sold all kinds of dishes such as pozole (pork stew with corn), enchiladas and carne asada tacos with fresh homemade corn tortillas.

On the day of the event, I was nervous, and, of course, the Queen was, too. At the beginning of the fiesta, the Queen made her entrance at 6:00 p.m. wearing a long pink dress, a tiara, and her white heels. She introduced herself and greeted the crowd. Then she performed a song. She received a standing ovation. The party had now begun. It lasted until 2:00 a.m.

The following day, the reactions of the people in the town were all positive. They stopped me on the street to congratulate me and told me it was one of the greatest events they had ever had. All those compliments made me feel very special. I realized that all my hard work had paid off. I gave this town something it would always remember. Not only was the day fun for all, but we also raised money for my class.

The second new event the town experienced was the end of the year graduation ceremony for my kindergarten students. Each of my 12 students performed. Some sang, some recited poetry and others danced. All the girls wore the same outfits made by one of the women in La Loma. The boys each wore black pants, a white shirt, a black tie and black shoes. Since some of the parents could not afford to buy the graduation outfits, I used some of the money we collected from the Spring Festival to buy the clothes.

I hired the same band that I used for the spring festival because everybody liked their music. The graduation began at 5:00 p.m. It started with the children holding hands, walking in a circle and saying hello to the audience. After each student performed, they paired up and danced a final waltz. I remember their parents' faces. Their jaws dropped as they watched in disbelief that their children could do all this.

Then it was time for me to say goodbye. Even though I wrote out what I wanted to say, when the time came I just said what my heart was thinking, all the great things that happened to me in their town. I kept talking in pauses because I was crying. When I was done with my "speech," I looked out into the audience and everybody was crying. And then the band started and the dancing began.

The next day I picked up all my belongings, went to the bus stop and left without looking back. Almost five years later, I returned to La Loma. As soon as I got off the bus, the word spread quickly that I was in town and everybody came to say hello. The moms told me that my special kindergarten class excelled in every grade which made me feel like I had done a good job. It has been 24 years since I became part of my students' lives and their families. I still remember each of them. We learned from each other. To me this was the greatest adventure a teenager could have. I enjoyed it and loved it!

Better Late Than Never

Aurelia D'Agostini

I was born in Italy in 1940, the fifth child of Armando and Rosario Raso. My mother had one more baby after me and we were a happy family. My father was a policeman in the village of Monasterace in the Province of Reggio Calabria, Italy.

When I was four my mother got an infection in the leg and without a doctor or hospital nearby, she became very sick. After a few months she passed away and life was not the same. My grandmother helped us to survive.

When I was eight my father became ill with pneumonia. With no medicine, he passed away. Then our lives really changed for the worse. We all had to start working, except my baby sister who went to live with the nuns. I had to go to work as a maid for rich people. It was very hard work for me and I was not treated well.

I never had a chance to go to school and learn to read and write until I was sixty. Thank you, Literacy Services, for changing my life!

Acknowledgements

Heartfelt thanks to the Carlsbad City Library and the sensational staff and remarkable volunteer tutors of Literacy Services. Your individual contributions and collective efforts enabled this publication. Also thanks to Denise Jessup, an Instructional Aide at MiraCosta College, for helping Gary Hailstone share his story.

Literacy Services Staff:

Carrie Scott

Deanna Westphal

Dennis Osgood

Helen Lindner

Judy Widener

Sandra Riggins

Taylor Tirona

Tiera Garfield

Tutors whose learners' stories appeared in this publication:

Ann Welch

Bruce Meyer

Chris Smoczynski

Jaime Morgan

Judy Gaitan

Lee Reich

Leigh Weatherwax

Lory McGregor

Louise Davis

Marie Tracz

Mary Lou Smith

Sandi Meyer

Sandy Zuris

Shirley Betters

Teresa Brady

Theresa Beauchamp